BLOOM COUNTY

Thirtieth Printing

Library of Congress Cataloging in Publication Data

Breathed, Berke
   Bloom County

   I Title
PN6728 B57B7   1983   741 5 973   83-5379
ISBN 0 316 10710 7 (pbk)

MV

Published simultaneously in Canada
by Little Brown & Company (Canada) Limited

PRINTED IN THE UNITED STATES OF AMERICA

INTRODUCTION
by Steve Dallas

Let me say right here and now that I never wanted to write this introduction. Fact is, the editors of this dubious tome originally sent out invitations for this very task to Dick Cavett, Leonard Nimoy, William Safire, Abbie Hoffman, Gary Hart, Steve Allen, Jessica Lange, Cathy Dillworthy, Jesse Helms, L. Ron Hubbard, Julia Child, Norman Lear, Erik Estrada, Oral Roberts, and Mr. T. All have thus far declined to even send a reply. (Actually, that's not entirely true. A large manila envelope was received containing an 8x10 glossy of what seems to be mostly a giant set of gleaming, capped teeth. It was signed, "To Miss Berp Breathit, All my love, Erik.")

At any rate, the editors (pretty darned frantic by this time) came to me at the last minute and said, "Here! Quick! Write a keen and clever intro, Dallas!" I said, "Forget it." They said, "Write the intro and we'll give you an '83 Buick jammed with tanked sorority girls with small noses!" And I said, "Who told you my weak spot?"

TAP TAP TAP

"Just tell how you have always loved reading the comics," they said. "And tell how you find them a perspicuous social barometer of contemporary living!"

I said, "Perspicuously speaking, eat the big one, boys. The only comic I read is 'Henry,' which hasn't any words. My kind of comic strip. Sometimes I'll look at 'Annie' because the hero, Daddy Warbucks, is an American war profiteer and damned well proud of it. My kind of comic character."

"For God's sake," the editors yelled, pulling at their bald spots, "don't write that! Be positive! Glowing! Gushing! Explain the comic page's relevance to the world at large."

"Okay," I said. "How's this? The funnies aren't more relevant than, say, the *New York Times* Op-Ed page, but they *are* more relevant than, say, plywood."

TAP
TAP TAP

Needless to say, more verbal ugliness was exchanged until the aforementioned promise of a gaggle of small-nosed sorority girls was nailed down, thus bringing us to the present with this keen and clever introduction, by yours truly.

At the outset, I should urge the squeamish and faint-hearted reader to approach the items contained in this volume with a certain amount of caution. As I am to understand the situation, these comic strips have been reproduced here in their virginal, unexpurgated form. That is, the original foul language has been brazenly reinstated after its earlier, careful excision by those more prudent and moral than Breathed.

It would seem appropriate, if not expected, at this point in the introduction to discuss the substance and subtle intricacies of the work at hand. It would, of course, only if I have read any of it, which I mostly have not, preferring, as I have already said, comic strips like ''Henry,'' which lack words. I said ''mostly'' just now because the truth is that I did indeed examine those particular *Bloom County* panels which included myself. Having done that, I can now report with some degree of confidence that they are all, bar none, totally libelous. And herein lies my biggest beef with *Bloom County* and all comic strips in general; accountability. Let's put it into bold caps: **ACCOUNTABILITY.** Or rather, the lack thereof.

People in Breathed's position don't have to answer to anybody. They work for no one newspaper and have no discernible superiors looking over their shoulders. Terms such as truth, objectivity and fair play mean diddly-squat to this crowd. Like young, smirking, pizza-faced hoodlums, they would explain their journalistic barbarities inflicted upon the likes of politicians, celebrities, clergy, close acquaintances and me with a mere shrug of the shoulders and wafting of open palms as they offer their shameful and legally effective defense of "Whoa! Just a joke, folks."

As an accomplished attorney at law, I can assure you that it would be infinitely easier to give Bella Abzug a hickey on the nose than it would be to successfully sue a cartoonist for libel. This peculiar condition of legal untouchability puts this bunch into about the same category as the Pope. This, of course, is entirely unsatisfactory, if not blatantly blasphemous. Thus, after careful consideration, I would urge that the entire population of cartoonists be rounded up like a pack of lame mules and shot.

TAP TAP
TAP TAP

Now, fully knowing that any keen and clever introduction should always include some insightful discussion about the author of the works being introduced, you will excuse me if the only relevant thing I can think of regarding said author is that while entertaining guests (me), he will remain rudely unconcerned about having an audibly flatulent Labrador named Boozer sharing the same room. Besides this, allow me to offer only the following deeply revealing morsel from his past for your collective consideration:

Item: On the summer afternoon of July 9, 1980, Berke Breathed was arrested, handcuffed and summarily convicted of harboring a live alligator in his one-bedroom Austin, Texas, apartment. He was briefly detained after being scolded, heavily fined and threatened with a jail term.

Two weeks later, Breathed was arrested again for harboring another alligator.

It is now, and obviously always has been, a problem of accountability with the guy.

Now. When do I get paid for this?

The Bloom Beacon

SENATOR BEDFELLOW TO VISIT BLOOM COUNTY TODAY

Miss Harlow's 4th Grade Class to be First Stop

"I love kids," says Senator Lucias Bedfellow. "The children are America's next great generation... can't wait to see what the little nips are like!"

GREETINGS... ANARCHY NOW!

BONK!

GOOD MORNING BOYS AND GIRLS!

GOOD MORNING SENATOR BEDFELLOW.

MY... SUCH A FINE GROUP OF YOUNG AMERICANS YOU ARE.

THANK YOU, SENATOR BEDFELLOW.

ANY QUESTIONS?

HOW'D YOU LAUNDER THE LIBYAN KICKBACK MONEY, SENATOR BEDFELLOW?

ANY QUESTIONS?

AW C'MON, SENATOR BEDFELLOW.

1

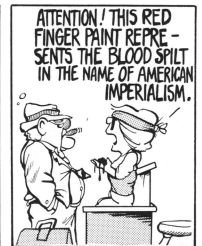

2

3

5

SPLENDID. I, CUTTER JOHN... NEW ARRIVAL TO THIS WILDERNESS CALLED BLOOM COUNTY, NOW FINDS HIMSELF HURTLING TOWARD OBLIVION SANS BRAKES...

OH GREAT. CONGESTION AHEAD. THIS IS GOING TO BE ONE ROTTEN DAY...

WOOSH!

COMING THROUGH!

OOPS. THINGS ARE LOOKING UP.

HEY!

WELL. HERE WE ARE. UH... LIVE IN BLOOM COUNTY LONG, BOBBI?

YES. WELL, NO... I MEAN JUST A FEW MONTHS, ACTUALLY.

OH, THAT'S NICE. UH... **OH FOR CRYING OUT LOUD!** LET'S STOP SMALL TALKING LIKE A COUPLE OF BLUSHING **TEENAGERS!**

OH, GAD! YOU'RE RIGHT. I **HATE** SMALL TALK! LET'S TRY TO GET TO KNOW EACH OTHER.

LEGS SHAVED?

HALFWAY.

AN
EVENING
OF
TELEVISION
AROUND
BLOOM COUNTY....

HI! I'M BROOKE SHIELDS AND I THINK PEOPLE WHO SMOKE ARE REAL LOSERS...BLECH!

PICKLES 10¢

THIS PROGRAM CONTAINS MATERIAL WHICH MAY NOT BE SUITABLE FOR YOUNGER VIEWERS. PARENTS, USE DISCRETION.

...AND PUT SOME LIFE INTO THAT DRAB MARRIAGE, LADIES! TOMORROW AFTERNOON, GREET YOUR HUSBAND AT THE DOOR WEARING NOTHING BUT A SMILE AND A BOTTLE OF CHAMPAGNE! BOY, WON'T HE BE SURPRISED!

K-TEL PRESENTS A '60'S COLLECTION OF MUSICAL CLASSICS JUST FOR YOU! WHO COULD FORGET JIMI HENDRIX'S "FREAKIN' IN THE PURPLE HAZE WITH A FLYING HIPPO?!..."

YOU. YES, YOU... ARE A SINNER. DON'T DENY IT.

OKAY.

8

AWRIGHT! I WANT TO KNOW EVERYTHING ABOUT THIS CLOWN YOU'RE SEEING!

FINE. HE'S CHARMING, EDUCATED, OPINIONATED AND IN A WHEELCHAIR, HATES SMOKING, LIKES—

HOLD IT. A WHEELCHAIR? HE'S IN A WHEELCHAIR?

RIGHT STEVE. SO?

WELL. SO... UH...

WELL IT'S HARDLY PREP.

I KNOW.

WHAT'LL YA HAVE?

A "TOM COLLINS"

A "HERRING WALLBANGER"

LOOK... I'M IN NO MOOD FOR YOUR DUMB JOKES, YOU STUPID WEIRD BIRD!

A THOUSAND PARDONS... IS SOMETHING WRONG?

YEAH. MY ROMANTIC AND SEXUAL LIFE IS IN TOTAL SHAMBLES.

OH.

SOMEBODY TELL ME WHAT COULD BE WORSE THAN BEING DUMPED BY A DAME FOR ANOTHER SCHLEP?

BEING EATEN BY A WALRUS.

GOOD EVENING. WELL, IT LOOKS LIKE CHRISTMAS WILL COME AFTER ALL THIS YEAR... DESPITE YESTERDAY'S FIRING OF ALL THE STRIKING "SANTA'S HELPERS" BY THE PRESIDENT....

IN A BIZARRE TURN, IT WAS ANNOUNCED TODAY THAT THE FIRED TOY MAKERS WILL BE REPLACED BY OUT-OF-WORK AIR-TRAFFIC CONTROLLERS.

THE $8 MILLION MAN

FOR THE REACTION TO TODAY'S ANNOUNCEMENT, WE GO TO PHIL JONES AT THE NORTH POLE... PHIL?

DAN, WE'VE GOT ONE UGLY ELF RIOT HERE...

AND THAT'S THE WHOLE STORY. THE GOVERNMENT FIRED THE STRIKING ELVES AND REPLACED THEM WITH THE FIRED AIR-TRAFFIC CONTROLLERS.

WELL, THAT'S RATHER SAD ABOUT THE ELVES.

DON'T WORRY. I WAS TOLD TO QUIETLY REHIRE MOST OF THEM.

REHIRE THEM? FOR WHAT?

HO! HO! HO! I'VE FIT THEM INTO THE OPERATION SOMEWHERE.

PUT IT IN GEAR DOWN THERE, LAUGHING BOY!

THESE NEW YEAR'S EVE PARTIES AT THE COUNTY CIVIC CENTER CAN BE **SO** TRYING...

HAP NEW

FEIGNED EXUBERANCE AND OVERINDULGENCE SEEM TO BE THE RULE OF THE DAY.

AS WELL AS JUST PLAIN GENERAL EXCESSIVENESS...

ALERT! THERE'S A SHRINER IN THE PUNCH!

ALL RIGHT, MILO.. WHAT'S GOING ON HERE ?

THE COUNTY NEW YEAR'S EVE PARTY, MR. ORACLE.

THIS IS PERFECTLY TERRIBLE! STOP THIS WICKEDNESS AT ONCE, I SAY!

= BONK!

THEY ARE LADEN WITH SPIRITS, AREN'T THEY KNAVE ?

PICKLED. TANKED. BLOTTO. YES.

18

21

22

23

24

25

27

EXCUSE ME. WE'D LIKE A PERMIT FOR A MASSIVE NUCLEAR WEAPONS PROTEST DEMONSTRATION AT COUNTY PARK.

HOW MANY PEOPLE?

CITY PERMITS

WE'RE HOPING FOR A QUARTER MILLION.

A QUARTER MILLION PEOPLE... RIGHT. NATURALLY YOU'VE ARRANGED FOR FOOD... PLUMBING FACILITIES...

CITY PERMITS

PLUMBING... YEAH. WE'VE ARRANGED THAT. WHAT'RE THOSE THINGS CALLED, BINKLEY?

CITY PERMITS

"PORTA-JOHNS"

YEAH. GOT ONE O' THEM.

CITY PERMITS

MILO, WHAT ARE WE DOING ON A COLLEGE CAMPUS?

RECRUITING. I READ IN "LIFE" MAGAZINE THAT THE NATION'S CAMPUSES ARE HOTBEDS OF LIBERALISM.

BUSI ECONC

BAN THE BOMB RALLY

HOTBEDS OF LIBERALISM?

HEY OVER THERE! YOU GUYS WANNA COME TO A NUCLEAR DISARMAMENT DEMONSTRATION?

BAN THE BOMB RALLY

SAY... LOOKIT THIS, JACK.

MIDGET COMMIES.

84

BAN THE BOMB RALLY

HOW OLD WAS THAT ISSUE OF "LIFE"?!

LET'S SKIN 'EM.

84

33

GREETINGS AND SALUTATIONS, SIR. PRAY TELL, WHAT IS THE PURPOSE OF YOUR MOBILE ALUMINUM GIZMO, HERE?

CUTTER JOHN

WELL IT SEEMS I'VE GOT A COUPLE OF USELESS LIMBS.

HELLO!.. DID YOU SAY "USELESS LIMBS?"

FLAP! FLAP! FLAP! FLAP! FLAP! FLAP! FLAP! FLAP!

BIRDS OF A FEATHER!

BREATHED

TODAY, MY SCIENCE REPORT IS ON THE EVOLUTIONARY ORIGINS OF THE PENGUIN...

CHAPTER ONE...

HOLD IT, BUB!

THERE'S A NEW STATE LAW AGAINST TEACHING PENGUIN EVOLUTION WITHOUT ALTERNATE THEORIES... WHAT'S THAT DRAWING, THERE?

CHiPs

A NEANDERTHAL PENGUIN

GET THE CUFFS, PONCH!

CHiPs

The Bloom Beacon

PENGUIN TRIAL STARTS TODAY

"PENGUIN EVOLUTION" VS. "SCIENTIFIC PENGUINISM"

WHAT SHOULD BE TAUGHT?

SO THIS WEEK THE COURT WILL DECIDE: DID PENGUINS EVOLVE THROUGH THE AGES OR WERE THEY CREATED IN NEWARK, NEW JERSEY IN 1912, AS ACCORDING TO SCIENTIFIC PENGUINISM?...

THE FIRST WITNESS FOR THE EVOLUTIONISTS WILL BE CARL SAGAN...

OKAY... SEE... BIIILLYUNS AND BIIILLYUNS OF YEARS AGO...

HOWDYA SPELL "BIIILLYUNS?"

YES SIR... ON FEBRUARY 1ST I GAVE A REPORT ON PENGUIN EVOLUTION TO MY CLASS.

MR. BLOOM... ARE YOU AWARE THAT WE HAVE LAWS REGARDING THAT IN THIS STATE?

WELL, I... UH...

OKAY! I DID IT! I KILLED HER HUSBAND AND DUMPED HIM OFF THE TRAIN OUTSIDE OF SHANGHAI!!

SORRY. WHAT WAS THE QUESTION?

I FORGOT!

35

MEET COREY SMITH... A COMMON MAN WITH DECIDEDLY UNCOMMON NIGHTMARES...

..FOR IN COREY SMITH'S MIND ARE MONSTERS...CREEPING DEMON REFUGEES FROM AN ALL TOO REAL IMAGINATION.

AND TONIGHT, COREY SMITH WILL COME FACE TO FACE WITH THOSE BEASTS FROM HIS HEAD...FOR TONIGHT, COREY SMITH WILL ENTER A PLACE WE CALL...

...THE TWILIGHT ZONE.

OH, MAJOR!

YOO HOO!

WHO'S THAT?

JUST US! YOUR HOUSE COCKROACHES!

HELLO! HELLO!

EAT DEATH, YOU DEVILS!

TUT! TUT! YOU'RE STUCK WITH US NOW, MAJOR.

THAT MEANS WAR!

NO, THAT MEANS ALICE HERE JUST LAID HER EGGS IN YOUR FRUIT-OF-THE-LOOMS.

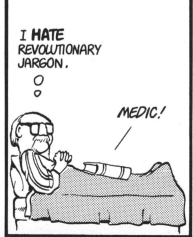

41

WELL, FOLKS, OUR LEAD STORY IS THAT THE **ROLLING STONES** ROCK AND ROLL GROUP WILL BE COMING TO PLAY AT OUR OWN BLOOM COUNTY ELEMENTARY SCHOOL DANCE.

NEEDLESS TO SAY, THIS NEWS IS STIRRING THINGS UP IN OUR OTHERWISE SLEEPY COMMUNITY.

REV. OTIS ORACLE HAS ADMITTED THAT NEXT WEEK'S **STONES** CONCERT **IS** CAUSING SOME CONCERN WITHIN THE LOCAL CHAPTER OF THE **MORAL MAJORITY**...

EVERYBODY SETTLE DOWN!!

IS IT THE APOCALYPSE? IS IT THE APOCALYPSE?!

THE BLOOM COUNTY **MOOSE** LODGE WILL COME TO ORDER. MEN... WE HAVE AN EMERGENCY. THE **ROLLING STONES** ROCK BAND IS COMING TO PLAY IN OUR VERY OWN COMMUNITY...

COMMENTS?

THEY WEAR WEIRD CLOTHES!

MAKE STRANGE NOISES!

AND ACT LOONY.

I PROPOSE A PROPOSAL TO CONDEMN THE WHOLE NASTY SITUATION...

ALL IN FAVOR MAKE THE SECRET MOOSE MATING CALL.

BLOOP! BLOOP! BLOOP! BLOOP! BLOOP! BLOOP!

42

HELLO?

MILO! THIS IS GOOBER MCGEE DOWN AT MY MOTEL! WHAT AM I S'POSED TO DO?

HAVE THE ROLLING STONES GOTTEN IN YET?

YEAH! AND STRIKE ME DOWN, LORD, I AIN'T NEVER SEEN NOTHIN' LIKE THIS IN MY ENTIRE LIFE!

WELL DO THEY LOOK GOOD? YA KNOW... RESTED?

WELL I CAN'T RIGHTLY SAY.

WEEKLY RATES

HEY, FOLKS! GOT A SURPRISE FOR Y'ALL TODAY HERE ON THE MORNING FARM REPORT!... MICK JAGGER OF THE ROLLIN' STONES MUSIC COMBO IS HERE FOR AN INTERVIEW!

WELL, MICK BOY...RECKON YOU KNOW THIS HERE'S PUT-NEAR THE CLOSEST THING TO A REAL TV SHOW THAT BLOOM COUNTY'S GOT.

FARM REPORT

FARM REPORT

GOT ANY SONGS 'BOUT HOG JOWLS?

FARM REPORT

LORD, YOU GAVE US FEET TO WADDLE, A TUX FOR TAILS AND BODS LIKE BOTTLES...

BUT 'SCUSE US IF WE FIND NO LEVITY, SINCE YOU ALSO GAVE US GRAVITY.

FLAP FLAP FLAP FLAP!

BUT TO ADVERSITY, WE SAY NUTS! AND WHEN IT'S TIME TO FLY THE COOP, WE FLAP AND BEAT TO LIFT OUR BUTTS...

...AND WE'RE LEFT AS WALKING NINCOMPOOPS.

SO LORD, I'D THINK YOU MORE THAN WISE, (AND ME MUCH LESS A JERK) IF ONLY ONCE YOU MIGHT SUPPLY...

...SOME PENGUIN WINGS THAT WORK.

HOWDY AND WELCOME BACK TO THE MORNIN' FARM REPORT, FOLKS. WE'RE TALKIN' TO THAT WILD **MICK JAGGER** FELLER.

YA KNOW, MICK BOY... YER LOOKIN' A MIGHT **LEAN** TO DO ALL THAT HOOTIN' N' HOLLERIN' AND JUMPIN' AROUND ALL DAY LONG...

FARM REPORT

NOW TELL ME, BOY... YOU EVER SAT DOWN TO A BIG OL' HEAPIN' HELPIN' OF FINE BLOOM COUNTY PIG LOINS AND CHICKEN GRITS?

FARM REPORT

'AVE **YOU** EVER SNORTED UP A FIFTH OF CHIVAS THROUGH A GUITAR NECK?

WHOA NELLY, NO!

FARM REPORT

POP... I'M OFF TO THE SCHOOL DANCE, NOW.

HMMPH.

THE ROLLING STONES WILL BE PLAYING.' GREAT, HUH?

YOU KNOW HOW I FEEL ABOUT IT.

THAT ROCK AND ROLL **SMUT** IS A THREAT TO THE TRADITIONAL MORALS OF THE **AMERICAN FAMILY!!**

POP, YOU THINK PANTYHOSE COMMERCIALS ARE A THREAT TO THE FAMILY.

GO. I DON'T CONVERSE WITH PAGANS.

45

49

50

EDUARDO! HOW GOES THE GLORIOUS COCKROACH REVOLUTION?

GLORIOUSLY, AHMED... GLORIOUSLY!

WE HAVE BROUGHT THE GREAT SUBURBAN SWINE TYRANT TO HIS KNEES!

YOU MEAN..?

YES! WE HAVE SEIZED HOSTAGES...

ONE MORE STEP AND WE LICK THE POT ROAST!

NO!

SENATOR? THIS IS MILO BLOOM AT THE BEACON. WILL YOU CONFIRM THAT YOU SUNK JIMMY HOFFA IN YOUR BACKYARD POND?

WHAT? OF COURSE NOT!

FINE. I'LL GO WITH "SEN. BEDFELLOW DENIES THAT POND IS WHERE HE SUNK HOFFA."

THAT'S NOT TRUE!

OKAY. "BEDFELLOW DID SINK HOFFA IN POND."

I DON'T KNOW WHERE HOFFA IS!!

"'I LOST THE BODY' SAYS BEDFELLOW!"

51

YOU WERE TALKING ABOUT THE TAX BILL, SENATOR.

OH YES...WELL NOW...UH...I VOTED THE STRAIGHT PARTY LINE ON THE BUDGET...

...'COURSE I TOLD O'NEILL THAT I COULDN'T SUPPORT A REVENUE BILL WHICH...UH... WHICH...

SAY, WHAT WAS I TALKING ABOUT?

THAT WILD PARTY IN HEFNER'S MANSION LAST NEW YEAR'S.

OH YES...

HELLO, SENATOR. THIS IS MILO HERE AGAIN AT THE BEACON. I NEED YOU TO CONFIRM AN OBITUARY NOTICE THAT WE'LL BE RUNNING ON THE FRONT PAGE TOMORROW.

MY SOURCE SAYS YOU DID. NOW... DID IT HAPPEN OVER AT YOUR MISTRESS' HOME?

WHAT? WHO DIED?

BUT I'M ALIVE!

I NEED A CONFIRMATION. CAN YOUR MISTRESS CONFIRM THIS?

I DON'T HAVE ONE!

"SENATOR BEDFELLOW. DEAD AT 65."

52

HERE IT COMES...

BILL the CAT

YES?

YOU'VE GOT A PIMPLE ON THE END OF YOUR NOSE.

OH FER CRYIN' OUT LOUD...

FOR THE LIFE OF ME, BOBBI, I CAN'T UNDERSTAND HOW YOU CAN BE SO DARNED UNROMANTIC IN OUR RELATIONSHIP THAT YOU'LL BLAB OUT SOME EMBARRASSING COMMENT ON MY PERSONAL APPEARANCE...

HEY...THE MAGICAL, PASSIONATE PHASE OF A LOVE AFFAIR IS SHORT ENOUGH WITHOUT RUSHING COMPLACENCY, RIGHT?

RIGHT?

HONEY, YOUR MUSTACHE SMELLS LIKE A CHILI DOG.

I WASN'T GOING TO SAY ANYTHING...

55

56

57

HI... I THOUGHT SOMEBODY OUGHTA LET YOU GUYS IN ON THIS...

ON WHAT?

YEAH. WHAT, MILO?

MILO'S MEADOW

NOW I DON'T WANT TO ALARM ANYBODY... BUT WE'VE HAD SOME RADIOACTIVE STEAM RELEASED INTO THE AIR FROM THE NUKE PLANT OVER THE HILL.

OH MY.

ON BEHALF OF MY SPECIES, I'D LIKE TO APOLOGIZE FOR THIS LITTLE faux pas.

SURE.

OKAY.

SO. CAN YOU GUYS STOP BREATHING UNTIL, SAY, TUESDAY?

OH MY.

TUESDAY?

YA KNOW, POP... SOME PEOPLE HAVE BEEN SAYING THAT WE OUGHTTA SHUT DOWN ALL THE NUKE PLANTS,

YEAH. RIGHT. THE COMMIES, THAT'S WHO.

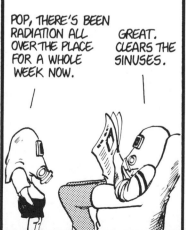

POP, THERE'S BEEN RADIATION ALL OVER THE PLACE FOR A WHOLE WEEK NOW.

GREAT. CLEARS THE SINUSES.

POP... THE CAT'S GONE BALD.

GOOD. SO HAS YOUR MOTHER.

59

AH'D LAHK TO WELCOME ALL YOU NEW INMATES TO OUR LITTLE PARADISE, HEAH... THE BLOOM COUNTY DOG POUND.

NOW IF THERE'S ANYTHIN' WE CAN DO TO MAKE YER STAY A MIGHT MORE COMFORTABLE, YA'LL JEST LEMME KNOW, HEAR? HEE! HEE!

ER... EXCUSE ME!

I'M AFRAID I DON'T MUCH CARE FOR THE DOG CHOW YOU SERVE. I'D LIKE TO REQUEST SOME FRESH, IMPORTED **HERRING.**

SON, WHAT WE GOT HERE... IS A FAILURE TO COMMUNICATE.

SAUTEED OR PICKLED... MAKES NO DIFFERENCE.

HI FELLAS... MIND IF I JOIN YOU?

NO RIOTING

HEY MAN... DIS IS DA WOLFHOUND TABLE. GO SIT WITH DEM UGLY POODLES OVER DERE.

WELL, THEY SAID I SHOULD SIT OVER HERE WITH THE OTHER "MANGY HAIRBALLS."

HEY SCUZBUMS! YOU GETTIN' DISRESPECTFUL OVER DERE?!

GO BITE A BONE, HAIRBALL!

ARF! ARF! ARF! ARF! BARK!! ARF!

I'LL JUST SIT OVER HERE.

HOW'S THE COCKROACH REVOLUTION GOING, FELLAS?

POORLY. THE SUBURBAN TYRANT KEEPS SMASHING US WITH HEAVY OBJECTS.

OUR CASUALTIES ARE RISING... OUR FREEDOM FIGHTERS ARE LOSING MANY OF THEIR LIMBS IN THE SKIRMISHES.

BUT NOT TO WORRY...WE ARE RECEIVING ARTI- FICIAL LIMBS FROM OUR COMRADES IN THE SOUTH.

A FLOW OF ARMS FROM NICARAGUA, EH?

SHH!

Bloom Beacon

BOOK BANNING DEMANDED

LOCAL GROUP TO PRESENT LIST OF "DANGEROUS" BOOKS TO SCHOOL BOARD

"BURN 'EM" SAY OTIS ORACLE

AND HERE, GENTLEMEN... HERE IS THE MOST DESPICABLE EXAMPLE... THE "ROGER TORY PETERSON FIELD GUIDE TO PENGUINS."

HERE...FOR ALL OUR CHILDREN TO SEE, ARE BIG GLOSSY PHOTOS OF HUGE MASSES OF THESE BIRDS UNABASHEDLY NESTING IN OPEN COHABITATION. NOW GENTLEMEN, I SUBMIT TO YOU...

...THIS IS PENGUIN LUST AT ITS UGLIEST!

I BEG YOUR PARDON.

66

67

71

73

AND SO... AS THE SUMMER WINDS ROLL IN OVER OUR LITTLE CORNER OF AMERICA CALLED BLOOM COUNTY, THERE COMES WITH IT SOMETHING NEW...

...NAMELY, A GROWING DISGUST WITH THE **ARMS RACE**. AND JUST AS IN COMMUNITIES EVERYWHERE, THE FOLKS HERE ARE GATHERIN' FOR ONE SIMPLE REASON...

...TO SOMEHOW GET THEIR MESSAGE ACROSS TO WASHINGTON...

TOWN MEETING TODAY

OKAY, THE CHAIR HAS BEFORE IT WIDOW PICKLEBY'S PROPOSAL TO FILL IN THE NEAREST NUCLEAR MISSILE SILO WITH HER SPECIAL, ZESTY BANANA PUDDING. ANY DEBATE?

BEFORE WE START, MR. BINKLEY HERE HAS AN ALTERNATE PROPOSAL FOR SOME GRASS-ROOTS ACTION AGAINST NUCLEAR WAR. LET'S GIVE IT A GOOD LISTEN.

TOWN COUNCIL

TONIGHT: NUKE ARMS FREEZE VOTE

OKAY. A GROUP OF US COULD SNEAK INTO THE PENTAGON ONE MORNING AND FLUSH ALL 760 TOILETS AT THE SAME TIME, EFFECTIVELY BURSTING THE PIPES AND MAKING THE ENTIRE AMERICAN MILITARY COMPLEX **HIGGLEDY-PIGGLEDY**.

TOWN COUNCIL

TONIGHT: NUKE ARMS FREEZE VOTE

THANK YOU. THAT BOGGLED THE MIND.

YEAH!

TOWN COUNCIL

NIGHT: KE ARMS FREEZE TE

THANK YOU AND GOOD NIGHT.

"HIGGLEDY-PIGGLEDY" MEANS "A REAL MESS."

TOWN COUNCIL

NIGHT: E ARMS FREEZE E

75

76

MEANWHILE... BACK AT THE BLOOM COUNTY DAILY BEACON...

WELL, OVERBEEK, YOU SHAMEFULLY SENSATIONALIST DOG, YER GONNA NAIL SENATOR BEDFELLOW TO THE SCANDAL WALL THIS TIME.

YEP! I'LL BET MY STAR REPORTER IS UNDERCOVER AND BAITING OUR PREY AT THIS VERY MOMENT...

WANT SOME DOUGH, O FAT ONE?

NO.

MY NAME IS ABDHUL. I WANT TO BUY PO-LITICAL FAVORS. TAKE THE DOUGH, BEDFELLOW.

YOU'RE MILO BLOOM AND YOU'RE FROM THE BEACON!

YOU ARE WRONG, O PORTLY ONE. I HAVE ARABIAN DRIVER'S LICENSE. HERE... HOLD THIS FOR A MINUTE.

OKAY.

FLASH!

Daily Beacon
BEDFELLOWSCAM!
CAUGHT!
PICTURES! WE GOT PICTURE

77

HEY, BINKLEY... I COULD USE A YOUNG, INNOCENT PERSPECTIVE SUCH AS YOURS ON SOMETHING.

WELL, I'D BE AS PLEASED AS PUNCH TO HELP, MR. DALLAS.

GOOD. LISTEN UP...

OKAY, THERE'S THIS DAME, RIGHT? AND I'M NUTS ABOUT HER. AND DEEP INSIDE I THINK SHE'S BONKERS OVER ME...BUT EVERYTIME SHE SEES ME, SHE CALLS ME AN "ELITIST *BOOB*." WELL, WHAT WOULD YOU DO?

SPIT IN HER MILK.

THANK YOU.

HI. NOTICED YOU FROM ACROSS THE BAR. YER CUTE. HOW 'BOUT HAVING DINNER WITH ME?

HUH?

THE SHOE'S ON THE OTHER FOOT, ISN'T IT? YOU JERK-FACE MEN AREN'T USED TO BEING ASKED OUT, EH? NO FUN, IS IT?

WELL...

SO HOW 'BOUT THAT DINNER? TUESDAY AT EIGHT. I'LL PICK YA UP.

LOOK... I, UH... I'M BUSY TUESDAY.

OKAY. MONDAY. I'M FREE ALL DECADE. I'LL CALL YA.

UH....

HE'S LOOKING FORWARD TO IT!

EXCUSE ME. WOULD YOU SAY THAT THIS IS AN INEVITABLE RESULT OF AN "IT'S-ALL-RIGHT-IF-IT-FEELS-GOOD" GENERATION? I'VE GOT FIVE BUCKS RIDING ON IT.

THERE THEY GO AGAIN. MISS HARLOW AND CUTTER JOHN ARE IN THE TALL GRASS MASHING LIPS.

IT'S WEIRD. TRULY IT IS.

IT SEEMS TO BE PURELY A MOUTH ACTION... A WIDE AND WILLFUL JOINING OF PUCKERED MANDIBLES....

COMBINED WITH A FORWARD THRUST OF THE FACE....

HOLD IT.

MUMPH GRDLUMPH.

YES, WELL, IT ISN'T TITILATING FOR ME EITHER.

81

I THINK I'VE GOT OL' STEVE DALLAS OFF MY BACK FINALLY. I SET HIM UP ON A HOT DATE WITH MY COUSIN TONIGHT.

YOU MEAN THE ONE THAT WANTS A PART IN "THE LOVE BOAT" SOMEDAY?

YEAH. HER NAME'S QUICHE LORRAINE.

QUICHE LORRAINE. WONDERFUL. I WISH I COULD BE THERE....

TELL ME THIS ISN'T 6684 POST OAK —

OH, PITS. IT'S NOT EIGHT ALREADY, IS IT?

UH... JUST SLIDE ON IN, QUICHE.

OW! I SIMPLY LOVE YER CAR!

YOU DO?

OH, IT IS ABSOLUTELY INTENSE! NEAT CARS JUST MELT ME!

A MAGENTA BUICK! PINSTRIPES...FAT TIRES... PIPES...MAG WHEELS... YOU MUST BE ONE SMOOTH MOVER! WHO ELSE WOULD OWN SUCH A FINE CAR?

WELL, MY OLD GIRLFRIEND USED TO SAY "ANY PIMP FROM POMONA" WOULD.

OH...OH...OH... A PLAYBOY DECAL... CATCH ME.

THERE'S THAT AWFUL CUTTER JOHN CLOWNING AROUND IN HIS WHEELCHAIR AGAIN. IT'S PERFECTLY DISGRACEFUL.

STOP IT! START TREATING YOUR DISABILITY WITH SOME RESPECT!!

WOOSH!

I THINK AN ALIEN HAS BEAMED ABOARD.

A KLINGON!

AN UGLY KLINGON!

ACK!

HELLO?! BLOOM BEACON?! THIS IS SENATOR BEDFELLOW! WHAT'S WITH THIS ★@#!! HEADLINE?

HEADLINE?

YES! THERE'S NO STORY... JUST A HEADLINE!

WHICH HEADLINE?

THE BIG HEADLINE ON THE FRONT PAGE!

READ IT TO ME, SENATOR.

"BEDFELLOW: THE SECRET LIFE OF A WIFE-SWAPPING ATHEIST"

OH, THAT'S JUST A TYPO.

HEY...THEY CAN'T COME IN HERE. THE HEALTH DEPARTMENT WILL CLOSE US DOWN.

EXACTLY, OL' BOY.

Sanders Fried Chicken

THEY'RE THE DELEGATION FROM THE MEADOW.. AND THEY'RE A LITTLE MIFFED ABOUT YOU SERVING THEIR FRIENDS AS FOOD.

BRETHED

WE'RE MAD AND WE'RE NOT GONNA TAKE IT ANYMORE !!

Sanders Fried Chicken

QUICK! GET ME A S.W.A.T. TEAM!

ALL RIGHT! LET'S DROOL ALL OVER THE PLACE!

Sanders Fried Chicken

WHAT'S GOING ON, OFFICER?

SOME RADICALS FROM THE MEADOW HAVE OCCUPIED THE FRIED CHICKEN RES- TAURANT...CLAIM THEIR FRIENDS ARE BEING SERVED AS "SNAK-PACS."

POLICE

GIVE IT UP !! EXTREMISM NEVER SOLVED ANYTHING!

BRETHED

POLIC

DEAR GOD, IT MUST BE GETTING UGLY IN THERE.....

POLIC

SUPPOSE THAT'S GEORGE?

COULD BE.

GEORGE ALWAYS HAD SUCH HEAVY THIGHS.

Kentucky Fried Chicken.

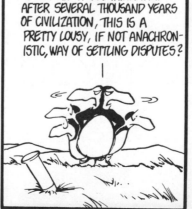

GIT OUT OF THERE!

MAJOR, DO YOU HAVE MOTHS IN THE CLOSET?

YES.

DO YOU HAVE COCKROACHES IN THE BATHROOM?

YEAH.

THEN PENGUINS IN THE FRIDGE WILL COMPLETE THE AMERICAN SUBURBAN EXPERIENCE NICELY, THANK YOU.

MOTHS IN...?

REFILL THIS WHILE YOU'RE THINKING. IT'S NESTING SEASON.

BREATHED

IS THIS THE LINE FOR THE NEW STEVEN SPIELBERG BLOCKBUSTER MOVIE?

YEAH.

"SPACE RAIDERS OF THE LOST EXTRA-TERRESTRIAL SHARK!"

BREATHED

DOES THIS FLICK HAVE ANY DISEMBOWELMENTS? FOR FOUR BUCKS I EXPECT DISEMBOWELMENTS.

ME TOO.

WHAT ARE WE HERE TO SEE?

A LITTLE SKIN!!

YEAH!

ONE PLEASE.

NO FLIGHTLESS SEABIRDS ADMITTED UNDER THE AGE OF TWO.

R

93

HEY.

YES, SIR?

WAS THAT YOU DOING THAT?

DOING WHAT?

SCREAMING DURING THE PREVIEW OF "SUPERMAN III."

SCREAMING WHAT?

"TAKE IT OFF, LOIS."

HE DID IT.

YA KNOW, I DON'T THINK CARY GRANT AND HEPBURN ARE WORKING TOGETHER WELL IN THIS FILM.

THEY'RE NOT IN IT.

WHOA. ISN'T THIS "THE PHILADELPHIA STORY?"

NO. IT'S "SPACE RAIDERS OF THE LOST EXTRATERRESTRIAL SHARK."

AND THAT'S NOT PHILADELPHIA?

IT'S PLUTO.

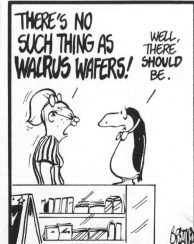

STEVE! DID YOU SEE THAT GUY MAKE THAT LEWD GESTURE AT ME?

SHUT UP. DON'T MOVE.

OH IT'S OKAY. "COSMOPOLITAN" SEZ IT'S ALL RIGHT FOR MEN TO BE PROTECTIVE AGAIN.

QUICHE... THE GUY LOOKS LIKE A DUMP TRUCK...

HEY, YOU BIG RHINO... MY BOYFRIEND IS GONNA SMASH YOUR NOSTRILS RIGHT THROUGH YOUR FACE!!!

OKAY. NOW POUND HIM. LIKE TOM SELLECK!

WHO?

"MAGNUM, P.I." I LIKE HIM TOO!

FOLKS MUST BE PRETTY HAPPY IN ENGLAND, LATELY.

Milo's Meadow

THE ROYAL LEGACY HAS BEEN PASSED TO YET ANOTHER GENERATION.

I THINK CHARLES MUST BE FEELING VERY PROUD AT THIS MOMENT...

DI... I THINK 'EE LOOKS LIKE... ME!

AND I'D LIKE TO JOLLY WELL SPEAK TO YOU ABOUT THAT.

OKAY. MY NAME IS STEVE DALLAS AND I'VE BEEN CONNED INTO BEING A SUBSTITUTE TEACHER FOR MISS HARLOW'S SUMMER CLASS THIS WEEK. NOW, ALL YOU LITTLE TERRORISTS CAN SIT DOWN AND SHUT UP.

HEY! WHAT'S ALL THIS?

AN INSPECTION OF NONVERBAL CUES, STEVE.

WE'VE LEARNED THAT CAREFUL SCRUTINY OF SUBTLE PHYSICAL CUES CAN TELL VOLUMES ABOUT A NEW PERSON.

OH YEAH? SCAT!

IMPULSIVE. MATERIALISTIC. A SELF-CENTERED BOOB. HIS FEET STINK.

HISTORY TIME, FOLKS. WE'RE GONNA LOOK AT AN ALL TOO OFTEN OVERLOOKED CHAPTER IN OUR PAST...

NAMELY, THE HEROIC ROLE OF FRATERNITY MEN IN AMERICAN HISTORY.

HEY. THERE'S NUTHIN' IN OUR BOOK ABOUT FRATERNITY MEN, STEVE.

SIDDOWN, BLOOM. IT'S IN THERE SOMEWHERE.

IT IS?

OKAY. "THE FAMOUS BOSTON FRAT PARTY." IN 1774, FRAT PATRIOTS DUMPED 168 KEGS OF LOW-CAL BRITISH BEER INTO THE —

WHAT PAGE?

FLIP. FLIP. FLIP.

98

"QUAKE"

QUAKE: Q-U-A-K-E.

"INNATE."

INNATE: I-N-N-A-T-E.

"CONSIGN."

CONSIGN: C-O-N-S-I-G-N.

"PSYCHOPHALLYSTISIS."

EAT HOT DEATH, STEVE.

SPELL IT, BLOOM. "PSYCHOPHALLYSTISIS."

FORGET IT. GIMME ANOTHER WORD.

LOOK... I'M RUNNING THIS SPELLING BEE

GIMME ANOTHER WORD OR I'LL GIVE THE LOCAL CABLE TV THE 8mm FILM I SHOT OF YOU LAST NIGHT BEHIND ED'S LUBE STATION GIVING QUICHE LORRAINE A SLOPPY HICKEY.

"EXTORT."

E-X-T-O-R-T.

EXCUSE ME, MRS. BEDFELLOW. I'M DOING A MAJOR PROFILE ON THE SENATOR AND I'M LOOKING FOR SOME INSIGHTS INTO HIS CHARACTER... MAYBE A FEW DETAILS OF HIS PERSONAL LIFE....

NO REPORTERS

PERSONAL DETAILS... OH MY. WELL... HE ENJOYS TAKING ME OUT FOR A QUIET WALK AT NIGHT... UNDER THE STARS... ENJOYING THE MOONLIGHT....

MOONLIGHT?

YES, THAT'S RIGHT.

WELL THEN. I GUESS I COULD PRINT THAT HE'S, WELL... KIND OF A "MOONIE."

OH MY! I THINK HE'D LIKE THAT!

GOOD EVENING. FRANK REYNOLDS HERE FOR ABC NEWS. TONIGHT'S TOP STORIES: THE U.S. ECONOMY RECOVERS... BANKS LEND MONEY FOR FREE.

OVERSEAS... THE SOVIETS ADMIT THAT COMMUNISM IS A TOTAL REPRESSIVE FAILURE. FREE ELECTIONS CALLED FOR NEXT TUESDAY.

AND JUST IN... COLUMNISTS GEORGE WILL AND BILL BUCKLEY CREATE A LEGAL DEFENSE FUND FOR GAY WELFARE CHEATS.

REALLY?

HA HA... NO.

I WASN'T GOING TO BUY THAT LAST ONE.

OKAY, CREW... LOOKS LIKE WE'RE READY TO START SHOOTING MY FIRST FILM... "E.P. — THE EXTRA-TERRESTRIAL PENGUIN."

IT'S A WARM AND SENSITIVE SCIENCE-FICTION EPIC FEATURING FANTASTIC SPACESHIPS, LEVITATING CHILDREN AND A WEIRD ALIEN PENGUIN.

NOW... WE CAN START SETTING UP THE FIRST SCENE IF OUR LEADING MAN IS BACK FROM WARDROBE.

I'M BACK. LET'S GO.

STEVEN SPIELBERG WOULD CALL THIS A "SPECIAL EFFECTS SPECTACULAR."

STEVEN SPIELBERG WOULD CALL THIS "LOW BUDGET."

MY DEAR SIR... IN THE CREDITS FOR "E.P. — THE EXTRA-TERRESTRIAL PENGUIN," YOU HAVE ME LISTED AS A "SPECIAL EFFECT...."

WELL, THAT'S WHAT'S WRONG WITH HOLLYWOOD!! ROBOTS! SPACESHIPS! SPECIAL EFFECTS! THE ACTOR IS FORGOTTEN! WELL, I WANT SOME CREDIT!

WHOA... HEY... I'M A REASONABLE MAN... LEMME JUST MOVE YA RIGHT UP HERE...

I'D APPRECIATE THAT.

AWRIGHT! LET'S SET UP THE NEXT SCENE!

OH, NOW THIS DOES SOUND BETTER... "KEY GRIP."

102

ALL QUIET ON THE SET! BINKLEY? IS THE SPECIAL-EFFECTS CREW READY FOR THE **CRASHING-SPACESHIP SCENE**?

I THINK SO.

OKAY. LIGHTS...SOUND... ACTION!

BLAM!!

WELL. I'M COMFORTABLY CERTAIN THAT SPIELBERG'S SPACESHIPS AREN'T FRISBEES AND SPARKLERS DIPPED IN GASOLINE.

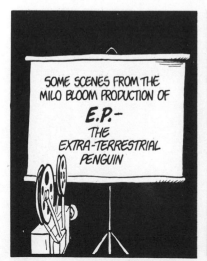

SOME SCENES FROM THE MILO BLOOM PRODUCTION OF

E.P.–
THE EXTRA-TERRESTRIAL PENGUIN

The interstellar spaceship lands

E.P. takes the boy flying

The final tearful farewell

103

STEVE...THIS SKINNY-DIPPIN' BUSINESS SEEMS DANGEROUS... WOMEN COULD BE LURKING IN THE BUSHES. REALLY.

KID, WHEN YA GOT A GREAT BOD LIKE MINE, YOU COULD CARE LESS.

WONDERFUL.

ALL I KNOW IS THAT IF ANYTHING EVEN SLIGHTLY FEMININE SAW ME NOW, IT'D BE...WELL....

TRAUMATIC?

YEAH. I'D PROBABLY RUN OFF AND BE A MONK OR SOMETHING.

WELL, HERE WE ARE, BINKLEY. THE FOUNDING FATHERS OF A BRAVE NEW REVOLUTION IN MUSIC...

YEAH.

SHUSH! REHEARSAL ZONE

MEADOW ROCK!

BEYOND NEW WAVE! UNADORNED, RAW AND SIMPLE ROCK!.. BACK TO THE BASICS!!

BACK TO THE BASICS!

'CAUSE BASICALLY WE ONLY KNOW TWO CHORDS.

WELL, THAT'S BASICALLY THE FACTS.

105

106

THEY DID IT! THEY LEASED THE MEADOW TO THE OIL COMPANIES!

JAMES WATT'S BEHIND IT!

EXXON'S MILO'S MEADOW

RIGHT! WATT'S BEHIND EVERYTHING!

WATT'S BEHIND THE OIL CONSPIRACY!

WATT'S BEHIND WORLD INDUSTRIALIZATION!

WATT'S BEHIND THE CANCELLATION OF "LOU GRANT!"

WATT'S BEHIND MY AUNT'S GOUT!

UH...

LET'S GO. WE'VE LOST THE MOMENTUM.

Restraint

Restraint

Restraint

DAD! WAKE UP! QUICK! DAD!

WHAT IS IT SON?

DAD! WILL BURT REYNOLDS EVER FIND "MISS RIGHT?" OR IS HE JUST TOO WILD AND FAST FOR ANY REAL STABILITY IN HIS LIFE?!

WELL? WHADDYA THINK?

YOU'VE GOT TO BE KIDDING.

MY FEELINGS EXACTLY... HE'LL SETTLE DOWN SOMEDAY.

MEANWHILE... OVER AT THE BLOOM BEACON...

BOSS... I'VE FOUND OUR NEW ENTERTAINMENT CRITIC.

HE'S A NATURAL. AND WHAT A VOCABULARY! GO ON... GIVE 'IM A TASTE, KID.

"FLOP." "A DISASTER." "TERMINALLY PUTRID..."

PRETTY GOOD. GOT ANY EXPERIENCE IN FILM, TELEVISION OR THEATRE?

NO.

GET THIS MAN A DESK!

"GEORGE PHBLAT'S NEW FILM, 'BENJI SAVES THE UNIVERSE,' HAS BROUGHT THE WORD **'BAD'** TO NEW LEVELS OF BADNESS."

TAP TAP TAP

"BAD ACTING. BAD EFFECTS. BAD EVERYTHING. THIS BAD FILM JUST OOZED ROTTEN-NESS FROM EVERY BAD SCENE...SIMPLY BAD BEYOND ALL INFINITE DIMENSIONS OF POSSIBLE BADNESS."

TAP TAP

TAP TAP TAP

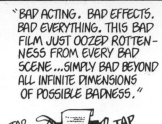

"WELL MAYBE NOT THAT BAD, BUT LORD, IT WASN'T GOOD."

HELLO! THIS IS FRANCIS FORD COPPOLA!

UH...HELLO MR. COPPOLA.

IS THIS THE CRITIC WHO REVIEWED MY NEW FILM "ONE FROM THE GUT" LAST TUESDAY?

MAYBE.

IS THIS THE CRITIC WHO WROTE THAT MY FILM "DID FOR THE MOVIES WHAT THE JONESTOWN KOOL-AID DID FOR KIDS' DRINKS?"

MAYBE.

I'M COMIN' ON OVER WITH A BASEBALL BAT.

SO I WAS A LITTLE GRUMPY TUESDAY....

OPUS! WAKE UP! YOU'RE HAVING ANOTHER DREAM!

YOU WERE SCREAMING SOMETHING ABOUT RONALD McDONALD CHASING YOU WITH A MEAT CLEAVER SINGING "McPENGUIN BURGER, EXTRA LETTUCE!... SPECIAL ORDERS DON'T UPSET US!"

I BET YOU FOLKS HAVE THAT SAME NIGHTMARE TOO, HUH?

CAN I HELP YOU SIR?

YES... UH...WELL... I WONDER IF YOU'D TELL ME ALL THE STUFF YOU SERVE HERE?...

SURE!

WE GOT McCHICKEN, McMUFFINS, McNUGGETS, BIG McMACS, QUARTER McPOUNDERS AND McFISHBURGERS. THAT'S IT!

WHEW! NO McPENGUIN BURGER?

McNOPE! BUT McMAYBE McLATER!

BURTON... I THINK THERE'S A PENGUIN SLEEPING NEXT TO US.

ZZZ... HMMPH... SNORT....

OKAY!! LET'S GET THIS PARTY STARTED!! BREAK OUT THE PERRIER! HEAT UP THE ASPARAGUS! WHO'S GOT THE ICE?!

OKAY, EVERYBODY... LET'S GET THE SINGLES PAIRED UP! SUZANNE SOMERS, YOU'RE WITH HARRY TRUMAN! CONGRESSMAN JOHNSTON, YOU'RE WITH ETHEL MERMAN... CHER, YOU'RE WITH...WELL, EVERYBODY.

AND YOU...WHAT ABOUT YOU, MADAM? ARE YOU WITH THAT MAN THIS EVENING?

AM I WHAT?

WITH HIM. ARE YOU TWO "INVOLVED?"

YES! YES WE ARE!

NO.

SHE'S LYING! THROW HER IN THE HOT TUB WITH AL HAIG!

GREETINGS! I'M HERE FOR MY BIANNUAL HAIRCUT!

WELL! JUST A LIGHT TRIM TODAY I THINK. WATCH THE BACK... I FAVOR A LITTLE FULLNESS AROUND THE FANNY...

..TRIM THE LASHES A TAD...CLIP THE NAILS... SHAMPOO MY TUMMY... THIN THE FLIPPERS AND SHAVE THE FEET.

AND THE NOSE HAIR?

OH JUST A LAYER CUT FOR THAT NATURAL, READY-FOR-ACTION DISCO LOOK.

WHHIRR...

THERE. HOW DO YOU LIKE IT?

OH MY. WELL. IT CERTAINLY IS A CHANGE, ISN'T IT?

LOOK...YOU WANT A HAIRSTYLE TO MATCH YOUR SINGLE, ON-THE-GO LIFESTYLE.

DO I?

YEAH. BABY, THIS IS YOU.

BUT WILL I GET THE CHICKS? I MEAN, IN TRUCKLOADS?

HELLO? BLOOM BEACON? — HELLO MRS. BILLSBY. HOW'S THE ARTHRITIS?

FINE, DEAR, BUT YOU FOLKS PRINTED THAT I DIED. — IMPOSSIBLE. WE DON'T MAKE MISTAKES ON THE OBITUARY PAGE, MRS. BILLSBY.

BUT I'M LOOKING AT IT RIGHT HERE. — OKAY...FIND SOME GOOD LIGHT AND READ IT TO ME SLOWLY.

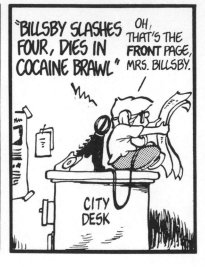

"BILLSBY SLASHES FOUR, DIES IN COCAINE BRAWL" — OH, THAT'S THE FRONT PAGE, MRS. BILLSBY.

RED ALERT! ALIEN SHIPS AHEAD! — QUICK! IDENTIFY THEM, MR. SULU!

"KLINGONS," SIR! — WRONG! THEY LOOK LIKE "ROMULANS" TO ME.

WELL, I SAY THEY'RE "KLINGONS." — THEY'RE "ROMULANS," SIMP.

SEEMS WE HAVE A CLASH OF IMAGINATIONS. — THEY'RE "KLINGONS." "ROMULANS." "HOTTENTOTS!"

115

RECENTLY, THERE HAVE BEEN COMPLAINTS THAT WE IN TELEVISION, MOVIES AND COMIC STRIPS HAVE BECOME MORE INTERESTED IN RAW COMMERCIALIZATION THAN ARTISTIC MERIT. FRANKLY, WE FIND THIS A **VILE** CONCEPT. WE HERE IN BLOOM COUNTY OFFER ONLY SOLID, UNCOMPROMISED ENTERTAINMENT... AND WE'D LIKE TO PROVE IT...

SO FOLLOWING A LONG TRADITION OF MOVIES AND PLAYS BASED ON COMIC STRIPS...WE BRING BACK OUR OWN "BILL THE CAT" TO SING A NUMBER FROM THE UPCOMING COLUMBIA FILM MUSICAL, "**BILLIE**." HIT IT, BILL!

OH, THE SUN WILL COME OUT... TOMORROW. YOU CAN BET YER TENDER VITTLES, TOMORROW!

TOMORROW! TOMORROW! I'LL CLAW YA, TOMORROW! ...IT'S ONLY A LITTER BOX AWAY!

WELL! THAT WAS SIMPLY WONDERFUL. NOT A DRY EYE IN THE HOUSE, I'LL BET.

SCRATCH! SCRATCH!

AGAIN, LOOK FOR "BILLIE" COOKIES, CLOTHES, WIGS, SHOES AND ASSORTED TOILETRIES IN FINE K-MARTS EVERYWHERE.

THAT DUMB SONG GIVES ME HAIRBALLS. GIMME MY 10% AND LEMME OUTTA THIS STRIP!

TODAY'S TOP STORIES: MORE VIOLENCE IN LEBANON... EL SALVADOR HEATS UP... IRELAND BLOWS UP... NEW WAR IN FALKLANDS...SOVIETS TEARGAS ENTIRE EASTERN EUROPE... BOMBS KILL PEOPLE HUNGER IN PAIN BLOOD DEATH

> CLICK. <

DANDELION BREAK.

"LIKE GRAINS OF SAND IN AN HOUR-GLASS GO THE DAYS OF OUR LIVES...."

REMEMBER, BINKLEY? REMEMBER WHEN WE USED TO CRAWL AROUND ON ALL FOURS...? AND BABBLE NONSENSICAL WORDS AND THROW OUR FOOD AT THE WALLS AND POUR MALT-O-MEAL ON THE CAT? REMEMBER?

NO.

AH...TO BE YOUNG AND FOOLISH AGAIN..

118

119

IN ORDER TO CLARIFY THINGS FOR NEW VIEWERS, DIM VIEWERS AND US, WE INTERRUPT THIS FEATURE FOR A QUICK REVIEW OF THE KEY PLAYERS ON THE TORRID **BLOOM COUNTY** ROMANTIC SCENE...

♥ QUICHE LORRAINE AND STEVE DALLAS ♥

QUICHE: DESIRES A ROLE ON "THE LOVE BOAT." SHE HANGS ON TO HER MACHO MAN, STEVE... WHO, BY THE BY, ACTUALLY HAS THE HOT BANANAS FOR SOMEONE ELSE..

♥ BOBBI HARLOW AND CUTTER JOHN ♥

HARLOW: SCHOOLTEACHER... WEARS ONLY EARTH TONES. SWEPT OFF HER FEET DAILY BY THAT CHAP THERE BEHIND HER.

♥ OPUS ♥

OPUS ISN'T SERIOUSLY INVOLVED WITH ANYONE WE'RE AWARE OF, BUT ASKED TO BE INCLUDED TO SHOW THAT HE'S STILL AVAILABLE.

SIR! WE'RE READY TO BOARD SHIP AND EXPLORE NEW WORLDS!

SORRY, CREW. NO MISSION TODAY.

DID YOU HEAR THAT, MR. SULU? SOMETHING MUST BE AMISS.

GRAB YER TRI-CORDER, SPOCK. LET'S TAKE A LOOK.

SNIFF SNIFF

WELL?

THE CAPTAIN... HAS A TOMATO.

CLEAR THE BRIDGE PLEASE.

120

121

GOOD DAY, MISS HARLOW. I HAVE A WONDERFUL INVITATION FOR YOU.

IT'S FOR AN EXCITING EVENING WITH MISTER STEVE DALLAS. THE DEAL INCLUDES A COUPLE OF CHEESE WHOPPERS, A GOOD SLASHER MOVIE ...

AND THEN A RIDE BACK TO HIS PLACE FOR A QUIET EVENING OF PECKING.

"NECKING."

...NECKING.

NO THANKS.

C'MON... FORGET ABOUT MISS HARLOW, STEVE...WHAT'S WRONG WITH QUICHE LORRAINE?

QUICHE. RIGHT.

THE WOMAN IS A WALKING VACUUM TUBE... SHE'S A VAIN, SELF-CENTERED, SHALLOW, BABBLING **BOOR**.

SO ARE YOU.

GET THIS...SHE PUTS MAKEUP ON HER **FEET**.

123

Meanwhile... over at the Daily Bloom Beacon....

AHEM!!

Where's the guy who wrote that I should be dipped in gravy train and thrown to a crazed pack of poodles?

Down the the hall, Senator

EDITORIAL DEPT.

AHEM..!

Down the hall.

CLASSIFIED ADS

Who is it, Opus?

Ronald Reagan.

EDITORIAL DEPT.

WHAT?

It's him. I think he's miffed about your editorial. Here.

EDITORIAL DEPT.

NO!! I don't want it! Uh... I'm not here! I'm not here!

I don't want it either! Here! Take it!

EDITORIAL DEPT.

Hello. Bert's Taco Palace.

ADIOS!

EDITORIAL DEPT.

...YES, MR. PRESIDENT...

EXCUSE ME. IS THERE A LADIES ROOM IN THIS BUILDING?

EDITORIAL DEPT.

OH, I AGREE, MR. PRESIDENT... THE EDITORIAL WAS IN THE WORST POSSIBLE TASTE... "ABOMINABLE." YES SIR. "INSULTING." YES SIR.

EDITORIAL DEPT.

WHAT'S THAT? YOU'D LIKE A FEW CHOICE WORDS WITH THE PERSON WHO WROTE IT?

EDITORIAL DEPT.

HERE.

FOR ME?

EDITORIAL DEPT.

GOOD EVENING. FRANK REYNOLDS FOR ABC NEWS. FOR TONIGHT'S TOP STORY, LET'S GO RIGHT TO SAM DONALDSON AT THE WHITE HOUSE... SAM?

♫ OH FRANK, GIMME DEM OL' HAPPY FEET... OO BOP-A-LOO-BOP! WANNA SHUFFLE ON DOWN PENNSYLVANIA STREET! BOO-BOP-A-LOP-BAM-BOOM! ♫

TAP TAP TAP TAP TAPPITY TAP.

I THINK SAM HAS FREAKED OUT.

FOLKS, EVIDENTLY SAM HAS FREAKED OUT.

125

Awake! Awake! But keep quite still!
SOMETHING'S MOVING IN THE MIDNIGHT CHILL,
FOR LATE AT NIGHT, WHEN THE CAT'S CAROUSIN'
THINGS COME OUT! THINGS COME AROUSIN'!

10-17

Just LOOK OVER THERE, DOWN ON THE FLOOR!..
A TEDDY BEAR SCREAMING "1984!!"
TEDDY BEARS USUALLY DO THIS, YOU SEE...
WHEN TEDDY BEARS ARE NAMED TEDDY KENNEDY.

And THERE! OVER THERE!
DOWN YONDER WAY,
IS MR. TIP O'NEILL
DANCING BALLET!
NOW SOME MAY CALL THIS
THE DANCE OF LEGISLATION,
BUT TIP IN A TUTU
IS A MORAL VIOLATION.

And OUT THE REST COME! FROM DEEP IN THE DRAWERS,
BAKERS, BYRDS AND KEMPS BY THE SCORE!
HOOTIN', HOLLERIN' AND JUST CARRYIN' ON,
LIKE SOME SORT O' CRITTERS DOWN
ON THE FARM!

BREATHED

But HEY, WHAT'S THIS? THE HAVOC WREAKING
HAS STOPPED 'CAUSE THE SUN IS PEEKING!
THEY RUN AND LEAP AND HIDE IN BUNCHES...
(NEED TO REST FOR THOSE THREE MARTINI
LUNCHES!)

YIKES!

Now IF YER WONDERING WHAT ALL THIS MEANS...
THESE SILLY SCENES MEAN JUST ONE THING...
POLITICS CAN BE QUITE FUN IT SEEMS,
IN COMIC STRIPS AND YOUNG BOY'S DREAMS.

1984!

IT'S ALMOST ELECTION TIME AGAIN! AND IF WE LOOK HARD, WE CAN SPY SENATOR BEDFELLOW AND HIS AIDE, STEVE DALLAS, STUMPING FOR THE MEADOW VOTE...

...AND SO IN CONCLUSION...

MILO'S MEADOW

...JUST BECAUSE MY CAMPAIGN HAS BEEN FINANCED BY THE N.R.A., THE AMERICAN HUNTING SOCIETY AND THE LEAGUE OF CRITTER SHOOTERS, I CAN ASSURE YOU, I HAVE EVERYONE'S INTEREST AT HEART!

QUICK...FIND SOME ★☺!?# BABIES TO KISS.

AND FINALLY, IF ELECTED, I CAN PROMISE PROSPERITY AND FREE BUICK ELECTRAS FOR ALL. FURTHERMORE...

MILO'S MEADOW

HONK!

HEY!

DAT WAS FER TALKIN' BULL PADDIES, BRO. NOW WHY DON'T YOU BOYS TALK STRAIGHT TO US JEST ONCE.

MY DEAR SIR... AS A DEDICATED PUBLIC SERVANT, I —

HONK! HONK! HONK! HONK! HONK!

127

NOW... I'LL TAKE SOME QUESTIONS FROM THE PRESS.

SENATOR BEDFELLOW... SOME PEOPLE ARE SAYING YOUR POLITICS ARE A DISGRACE. ANY COMMENT?

NO.

SENATOR... SOME PEOPLE ARE SAYING YOU SELL NUDE BARBI DOLLS ON THE SENATE FLOOR. COMMENT?

WHO'S SAYING THAT?!

I DUNNO. I SURE AM.

IS ANYBODY SAYING THAT?

SENATOR, SOME PEOPLE ARE SAYING YOUR WIFE RIDES WITH BIKERS...

GOOD MORNING. BLOOM BEACON.

THIS IS SENATOR BEDFELLOW... WHAT HAVE YOU HACKS GOT PLANNED FOR ME TODAY?

SENATOR, BEING THE RESPECTABLE JOURNAL THAT WE ARE, WE WOULD HARDLY EDITORIALIZE ABOUT A CANDIDATE ON ELECTION DAY.

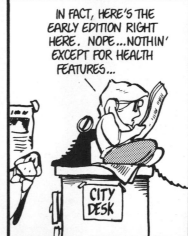

IN FACT, HERE'S THE EARLY EDITION RIGHT HERE. NOPE... NOTHIN' EXCEPT FOR HEALTH FEATURES...

ELECTION DAY

Bloom Beacon

DOCTORS WARN: VOTING FOR BEDFELLOW LEADS TO HERPES

128

NEWS, DAD. BURT REYNOLDS AND LONI ANDERSON ARE OFFICIALLY A HOT ITEM.

YA KNOW, MOST OF US AGREED THAT DINAH SHORE WAS NO GOOD FOR BURT... BUT WE DID **NOT** FEEL THAT HIS DUMPING OF POOR SALLY FIELD WAS MERITED IN THE LEAST.

CAN LONI MAKE HIM HAPPY? OF COURSE NOT. AND DINAH IS STRICTLY YESTERDAY'S PAPERS. I THINK HE SHOULD GET A GRIP ON HIMSELF AND MARRY SALLY. WHAT DO YOU THINK?

I THINK HE SHOULD AVOID HAVING A SON.

BURT, OH BURT... ALWAYS THE FREEWHEELING AQUARIUS.

SAY...ISN'T THAT THE NEW GIRL FROM L.A.? WELL! THIS **IS** A PLEASANT SURPRISE!

STEP ONE...WE NEED A SMOOTH LINE FOR THIS LITTLE HOT PEPPER.... SOMETHING TO KNOCK HER OFF HER GUARD AND INTO YOUR LIFE...

SOMETHING NICE... ROMANTIC YET FIRM... SENSITIVE, YET STILL MACHO...OKAY... *BOMBS AWAY!*

WOULD YOU LIKE TO SHARE SOME NASAL SPRAY?

OKAY. STEP TWO...

THE "OPUS FUN PAGE" PRESENTS THE '83 SPRING FASHION GUIDE ★

"WILD" IS THE WORD IN FASHION ON TODAY'S TURBULENT CAMPUS SCENE!.. YES, RALPH HERE IS DRESSED TO JOIN THAT HOTBED OF REBELLION: THE AMERICAN CAMPUS, 1983. HE LOOKS SPIFFY IN HIS LEVI'S "MOVIN' ON" JEANS AND "BILL THE CAT" T-SHIRT. HAIR BY "COMMAND PERFORMANCE."

TAKE OFF, EH?

YOO HOO!

E.T.

THE LIGHT AND BREEZY LOOK FOR THE DISCRIMINATING CULTIST... HAMSÜJTA IS LOOKING PERKY AS HE POUNDS THAT HOT AIR-PORT PAVEMENT IN HIS PINK "DHOTI" ROBE AND LLAMA BEADS. A SILK TIE BY BILL BLASS ADDS JUST THAT RIGHT TOUCH OF RESPECTABILITY. HAIR BY GILLETTE SAFETY RAZOR.

FOR THE FASHION CONSCIOUS TV EVANGELIST, THE WORD FOR '83 IS STILL "LOUD..."

HERE'S REV. TOMMY JOE BAKKER LOOKING SNAPPY FOR THE CAMERAS IN HIS FASHIONABLY LOUD SUIT, LOUD HAIR, LOUD TIE AND LOUD POLITICS. AS A MATTER OF FACT, NEARLY EVERYTHING ABOUT TOMMY JOE IS LOUD EXCEPT FOR HIS BANK ACCOUNT...THAT'S KEPT PRETTY QUIET.

FOR THE DISCRIMINATING PENGUIN, THE WORD IN FASHION IS STILL "YECH!" BECAUSE PENGUINS LOOK TERRIBLE IN NEARLY EVERYTHING...SO WE'LL JUST MOVE ON.

WHAT? BUT I'M ALL READY! HEY!

HEY BABY!

YOW!

PUNK PREP! THE BEST OF BOTH WONDERFUL WORLDS FOR YOU MODERN GALS!

HERE'S "MAD DOG" KITZI READY FOR A BIG SHOPPING DAY AT SAKS... COMBINING THE RAW SEXUALITY OF ARGYLE KNEE SOCKS AND RIBBON TIES WITH THE DOWN-TO-EARTH SENSIBILITIES OF A MOHAWK HAIRDO, KITZI IS JUST ONE HELL OF A MAN-PLEASER ALL THE WAY AROUND!

BOY...THE HISTORY OF U.S. DIPLOMACY CERTAINLY IS A PATCH-WORK OF PERSONALITIES...

FROM KISSINGER TO AL HAIG...THE DIVERSITY IS DRAMATIC...EVEN STARTLING...

JUST TAKE CYRUS VANCE...A STUDIOUS, GENTLE DIPLOMAT... WOULD YOU LIKE TO GO TO A MOVIE WITH ME?

SURE.

THEN THERE'S OL' GEORGE SHULTZ... STRICTLY A "TEAM PLAYER." I'M BROKE, SO CAN WE GO DUTCH?

DAD, I'VE MADE A DATE WITH THE MOST BEAUTIFUL GIRL IN THE ENTIRE KNOWN UNIVERSE.

MY SON IS IN LOVE!

HER EYES... LIKE BIG WIDE CHESTNUTS! AND HER LITTLE NOSE... LIKE A CUTE BUTTON MUSH-ROOM!

AND HER SKIN... LIKE SMOOTH AND CREAMY CHOCOLATE PUDDING.

"CHOCOLATE?"

FUDGE. WHATEVER.

134

..SO THE AGRICULTURAL FORECAST FOR SPRING LOOKS GOOD. CORN UP TWO POINTS... WHEAT UP THREE... SOY BEANS DOWN ONE BUT RICE UP FOUR.

Z.

PENGUIN FEET UP TWO.

HMPH? HUH? WHAT?

NOW **STAY** AWAKE!

THE BOYS DOWN AT THE FARM REPORT ARE GETTIN' A MIGHT TESTY.

DAD! WAKE UP! QUICK! THE SITUATION IS CRITICAL!

BURT REYNOLDS, DAD! IS THE WRITING ON THE WALL FOR BURT?! TOM SELLECK IS COMING UP FAST, YA KNOW! WHO'LL COME OUT ON TOP, DAD?!

AND ERIK ESTRADA! LET'S NOT FORGET ERIK ESTRADA! YOU KNOW WHAT **HE** IS, DON'T YA, DAD!

I DUNNO.

OUR YARD MAN?

NO! THE **WILD CARD!** COULD ERIK BE THE NEXT "HEAD HUNK?" MY GOD, IT'S UTTER CHAOS!!

SIR! I UNDERSTAND YER IN CHARGE OF THE FUNNY PAGES AT THIS NEWSPAPER!

WELL I GUESS I AM.

The Bloom Beacon

GREETINGS! I REPRESENT THE **UNIVERSALLY UNITED WRITERS BUNCH** SYNDICATE. AL McMEED IS THE NAME AND COMIC STRIPS ARE THE GAME!

U.U.W.B

FEATURES DEPT.

YEP! I GOT WHAT YOU WANT! STRIPS ABOUT DIVORCE! STRIPS ABOUT BABIES! STRIPS ABOUT PLUMBERS! STRIPS ABOUT DIVORCED **BABY PLUMBERS!**

U.U.W.B

FEATURES DEPT.

HOW 'BOUT ANIMALS? YA LIKE ANIMALS IN COMIC STRIPS?

NO.

FEATURES DEPT.

...LOOK...TODAY'S COMICS GOTTA TARGET SPECIFIC MARKETS! NOW *HERE'S* A HOT NEW STRIP FER THE "COW LOVERS" MARKET...

FEATURES DEPT.

...IT'S CALLED "THE GOSSIPING COWS!" SEE, THERE'S THIS ONE COW THAT'S ALWAYS ASKIN' "WHAT'S NEW?" AND THE OTHER COW IS ALWAYS SAYIN' "UDDERLY NOTHING!"

FEATURES DEPT.

GET IT!? "UDDERLY!" HA! HA! I'M DYIN'!

MIGHT YOU HAVE A STRIP WITH A PENGUIN IN IT?

FEATURES DEPT.

PENGUINS? NAW...STINK LIKE ROTTEN FISH. NO MARKET FER THAT.

OH DEAR...

FEATURES DEPT.

138

SIR?.. SIR! HEY...C'MON. DON'T SWITCH TO ANOTHER NETWORK. THIS IS GRANT TINKER OF NBC... THE QUALITY NETWORK.

LOOK, OUR RATINGS HAVE BEEN IN THE DUMPS FOR 96 MONTHS NOW, YET WE ALWAYS CLEAN UP AT THE EMMYS... NOW I'M NOT SURE WHAT'S GOING ON, BUT I DO KNOW THAT, DEEP DOWN, THE AMERICAN TV PUBLIC CRAVES JUST ONE THING...

...BRIGHT, INTELLIGENT ENTERTAI——

CLICK

GILLIGAN!! DROP THOSE COCONUTS!

BONK!

OW!

SLURP SLURP

WHEAT THINS

BINKLEY... SOMETIMES I THINK THAT LIFE AROUND HERE IS JUST TOO DULL... BORING...NORMAL...

MILO'S MEADOW

HIDE THE WOMEN! THE RUSKIES ARE COMING! THE RUSKIES ARE COMING!

MILO'S MEADOW

QUACK! QUACK! QUACK! QUACK! QUACK! QUACK!! QUACK! QUACK! QUACK! QUACK!

MILO'S MEADOW

...MONOTONOUS... HUMDRUM...

WAIT UP, COMRADES!

NO!! JUST ONCE LEAVE IT ON NBC! WE'VE GOT INTELLIGENT, PROVOCATIVE HOLIDAY SPECIALS UP NEXT!.. JUST LISTEN:

"NORTH POLE BLUES".. A TOUGH, UNFLINCHING LOOK AT THE TRAUMAS AND TRIUMPHS OF THE GRITTY LIFE AT SANTA'S WORKSHOP. WATCH "RENKO," THE UPPITY ELF WHO... WHO...

HEY... WHAT ARE YOU DOING? DON'T! THIS IS CLASS MATERIAL —--!!

CLICK!

..WELL TATTOO, MR. FINCH'S FANTASY IS TO SWAN DIVE INTO A BOWL OF EGGNOG WITH BARBI BENTON.

OO DAT'S NICE, BOSS!

NOW WE'RE COOKIN'!

THERE'S PANDEMONIUM BACKSTAGE AT THE BLOOM COUNTY SCHOOL AUDITORIUM! THE CHRISTMAS PLAY IS ABOUT TO BEGIN..

WE'LL NEVER MAKE IT... THE SET CAUGHT FIRE... OUR SHEPHERDS ARE ALLERGIC TO FAKE SHEEP... WHAT NEXT?

PROPS

DIRECTOR

SIR! OUR THREE WISE MEN ARE DOWN THE BLOCK PLAYING MS. PAC-MAN!

WHAT? WELL GO GET 'EM!

SIR!

WHAT?

THE STYROFOAM COW IN THE MANGER SCENE JUST GOT SMOOSHED BY A TRUCK IN THE ALLEY!!

BRING IN THE COW'S UNDERSTUDY!!

THE A.C.L.U. IS BEHIND ALL THIS.

140

148